TEESDALE
IN OLD PHOTOGRAPHS

EX LIBRIS

E.T . FRETWELL

A PHOTOGRAPH OF A PAINTING by Jacob Readshaw (see page 104) showing the old house at Middle Crossthwaite, Holwick. A farm diary of 1872 notes that the family living there would have to be rehoused because the building, especially the thatched roof, was in a very bad state of repair. The picture must have been painted not long before this date. The house is now a barn.

TEESDALE
IN OLD PHOTOGRAPHS

COLLECTED BY
DENIS COGGINS

ALAN SUTTON
1989

Alan Sutton Publishing
Gloucester

First published 1989

British Library Cataloguing in Publication Data

Teesdale in old photographs.
1. Durham (County). Teesdale, history
I. Coggins, D.
942.8'61

ISBN 0–86299–608–2

Typesetting and origination by
Alan Sutton Publishing
Printed in Great Britain by
Dotesios Printers Limited

CONTENTS

INTRODUCTION   7

1. THE ENVIRONMENT   11

2. TOWNS AND VILLAGES   19

3. BUILDINGS   29

4. WORK   51

5. ROAD AND RAIL   79

6. PEOPLE   99

7. LEISURE   119

8. OCCASIONS   129

9. VISITORS   149

    ACKNOWLEDGEMENTS   160

THIS ELABORATE LIMESTONE TOMB which had been removed to Rokeby Park has since been restored to its original place in Egglestone Abbey.

MR RICHARD PRATT, a gamekeeper, with his family outside their home at Loups, Cotherstone, now derelict.

INTRODUCTION

Teesdale District is by far the largest of the local government districts in Durham County but has much the smallest population. It is bordered to the west by Cumbria, to the south by North Yorkshire, to the north by Wear Valley District and joins Darlington on the east. The district, as it exists today, is the creation of the local government reorganization of the 1970s which amalgamated three groups of parishes whose historical backgrounds were different.

Whatever the position in prehistoric or Roman times may have been, from the early medieval period onwards the river Tees formed an important boundary. This was respected when estates were redistributed after the Norman Conquest. The manor of Gainford, which extended along the north bank of the Tees 'to the mountains in the west' – as an early charter phrased it –, was given to the Balliol family who later made the newly-built Barnard Castle their headquarters. The villages to the south of the river, most of which were described as 'waste' in the Domesday Book, formed part of the enormous honour of Richmond, given to the Dukes of Brittany. Throughout the medieval period the Bishops of Durham tried repeatedly to add Teesdale to their extensive possessions to the north and east which included townships such as Evenwood. Apart from brief periods when they were held by the Crown, the lands north of the river have been the possessions of only three successive families: Balliol, Neville and – since the Civil War – Vane.

Administratively they have formed part of the County of Durham. To the south of the river, in the North Riding of Yorkshire, it was the Bowes family which became the principal landowner. Thus, during the period covered by this book, most of Teesdale was owned by the Dukes of Cleveland and the Earls of Strathmore.

These political divisions did not reflect any real geographical distinctions between the two banks of the river and the present situation which stresses the unity of Teesdale is, in this respect at least, much more practical.

The scenery of Teesdale and its botanical importance were appreciated long before photography began to record them. The botanists recognized the rare flora some time before the kind of rugged wildness characteristic of the upper part of the dale was appreciated by tourists. A vicar of Brignall in the seventeenth century was a nationally known naturalist while, during the next century, Hunter and Ray began the descriptions of the Teesdale rarities, work which was later carried on by a lead-miner, Binks. Arthur Young, secretary of the Board of Agriculture visited Teesdale in 1770 and described it in glowing terms but it was, perhaps, the paintings of Turner and the poems of Scott which began to popularize the dale. The anonymous author of a *Tour in Teesdale* could still write in 1828 '... my design is ... to give Teesdale its due place and character in picturesque scenery; and to induce the Naturalist as well as the Tourist to explore a country almost new to their different purposes ...'.

But even as this was happening Teesdale was changing. Until the end of the eighteenth century the economic basis of Teesdale was, as everywhere else, essentially agricultural, although coal, iron and lead had been worked in small quantities since Roman times. The intensification of the lead industry which resulted from the arrival of the London Lead Company in the mid-eighteenth century changed things dramatically. The population increased rapidly as men and sometimes whole families arrived in the dale to seek work in the mines. There was also a steady stream of young women from Westmorland and Cumberland taking jobs as farm or domestic servants. Often they married and remained in Teesdale. The primacy of the lead industry is shown by an example taken at random from the Middleton parish registers: in 1837 there were 113 baptisms and in 83 cases the father's employment was mining or smelting. The occupations of the fathers of the 12 illegitimate children are not given. Despite, or because of, the 'enlightened' attitude of the Company, little of the wealth created went to its workmen, although the communities in general benefitted greatly and the Dukes of Cleveland benefitted even more with some £9,000 p.a. in royalties. Some of this was, however, returned to the dale by the creation of smallholdings for miners.

In the third quarter of the nineteenth century the price of lead began to fall and mine after mine closed down. By 1900 leadmining had virtually finished. Miners were forced to seek work elsewhere. From around 1850 onwards the coal mines of Evenwood, Cockfield, Butterknowle and Woodland increased in numbers and production, especially after the railway network made it possible to transport coal over long distances. Many lead-miners sought work in the coal pits. Others emigrated. From 1871 onwards information for intending emigrants was published weekly in the *Teesdale Mercury* and in 1880 the paper noted '... never have so many emigrants left Barnard Castle ...' The town itself had high unemployment because of the collapse of the carpet-weaving industry. To some extent quarrying took the place of lead-mining in the upper dale but the population continued to decline towards its pre-1750 figures. The coal-mining areas, however, were booming with new colliery houses being built everywhere and immigrants arriving to seek work. Their decline did not come until the 1920s.

The arrival of the railway made possible the expansion of coal and stone production. It also made practicable closer connections between Teesdale and the world outside. In July 1867 for example, over 600 people, most of them children, left Barnard Castle station for a day trip to Sunderland. They included pupils from Middleton schools who had left at 3 a.m.! Day excursions in the reverse direction were enormously popular for years and gave many of the people of Sunderland their first taste of the countryside, beginning a connection which continues today.

The wealthy shooting tenants of the grouse moors found that they could travel up from (or should one say 'down from'?) London for a few days at a time. When the Prince of Wales visited Holwick moors in 1866 he was able to stay for a week before, as reported by the *Mercury*, '. . . at half past eleven *pm* H.R.H. left in a bus from Mr. Smith's King's Head Hotel, Barnard Castle for the railway station at Lartington, passing through Middleton where a loyal crowd had assembled to give the Prince a parting cheer . . .'

On a more mundane but more useful level, a farmer's diary of 1872 shows that it was possible for him to leave home at Holwick, travel to Penrith and return with some sheep, something quite impossible by public transport today. This, then, is very briefly the background to this book. Photography arrived too late to capture the early years of the local industrial revolution or, unfortunately, the rural society which preceded it. The heyday of both lead and coal was, however, recorded and is dealt with only in outline here because it has been done much more fully and accurately elsewhere.

The choice of photographs and the interpretations put on them are very much a personal matter made within the constraints imposed by the availability of the material. There are many omissions, some intentional, others because of the author's ignorance and some perhaps because the relevant photographs do not exist.

The arrangement of the photographs in sections is again an arbitrary one and I am sure that other people would have chosen different headings, while some photographs could have appeared in more than one section. I hope that despite its shortcomings this selection of photographs will, to those who do not know Teesdale at all or know it only as it is now, give a little of the character of people, times and sometimes places, that are gone. To those who know more about the subject than I do, I can only apologize for not doing a better job.

On 21 April 1969 the *Teesdale Mercury* ended the last of a series of articles on local historical topics with these words:

'. . . it is possible that a scrutiny similar to that which the files of an early Barnard Castle printer have undergone at our hands may be given to these pages. If so we trust that the explorer may have the same amount of gratification we have had and that . . . he also may have to say that the time in which he lives is better than any other that preceded it . . .'

Let us hope so.

The Environment

FOR MANY PEOPLE from all over the world Teesdale means the spectacular waterfall of High Force, the biggest fall in England, seen here from the cliffs on the south bank of the river.

THE RIVER TEES has its source high on Cross Fell and, for the first ten miles of its course, flows through some of the wildest moorland in the country. Before the reservoir was built at Cow Green the river meandered slowly across the floor of a peaty basin forming a long still pool known as the Weel. This was the 'Cauldron' over the basalt lip or 'Snout' of which the river poured in a spectacular cascade for over 200 ft. The Cauldron Snout waterfall is still there, although the footbridge shown on the photograph has been replaced by a more substantial road bridge, but the Weel, said to have provided the inspiration for Samuel Palmer's painting *The Plains of Heaven*, has gone for ever.

THE GEOLOGICAL FEATURE known as the Great Whin Sill responsible for the falls of High Force and Cauldron Snout outcrops at several places in the dale, most spectacularly here at High Cup Gill on the extreme western edge of Teesdale, overlooking the Eden valley in Cumbria. The stream in the foreground eventually joins the river Eden.

THE RIVER TEES is still liable to sudden rapid rises in level which can be dangerous to the unwary. Before the construction of the Cow Green reservoir these floods were more common and more severe. Occasionally, as here in 1968, a combination of heavy rain and melting snow can still cause spectacular floods. The photograph looks upstream with the bridge at Cronkley in the middle distance. Though not perhaps to be compared with the great flood of 1771 it nevertheless caused extensive damage throughout the dale.

THERE ARE MANY WATERFALLS on the tributary becks in the upper dale. One such, now much frequented by visitors to the nearby Bowlees Interpretative Centre, is Gibsons Cave on the Bowlees beck. Here the water has eroded underlying shale beds more quickly than the harder limestone above forming a shallow cave behind the fall. Tradition makes this the hiding place of an outlaw named Gibson but there seems to be no real evidence for this.

THE RIVER LUNE, which joins the Tees just below Middleton, was once a major tributary but its flow is now controlled by reservoirs, the first of which at Grassholme was built around the turn of the century, submerging the sites of the farms and mill seen here. The bridge was not demolished and can occasionally be seen when the reservoir is low.

THE 'BOULDER STONE' lies on the north bank of the Deepdale Beck which joins the Tees at Barnard Castle. It was a favourite destination for Sunday afternoon walks, school visits and picnics. Teesdale was heavily glaciated during the last Ice Age: one glacier originated in the high fells at the head of the dale, joining another from the Cumbrian hills. The latter brought with it many boulders of shap granite like the one in the photograph.

THE RIVER GRETA, which rises high on Stainmore and is seen here at Bowes, is another tributary of the Tees. 'Greta woods', Sir Walter Scott's heroine assured us, 'are green', adding that she would 'rather rove with Edmund there than reign our English queen'. It is indeed a beautiful river. The building in the distance has, like so many of the watermills, been long demolished though the mill race can still be traced.

THE RIVER GRETA (in the foreground) joins the river Tees near Rokeby at the romantically named Meeting of the Waters. This beautifully composed photograph and the two which follow are the work of E. Yeoman who worked in Barnard Castle around the turn of the century. Although in summer the Greta flows very quietly through its limestone gorge here, in winter it can become a torrent deafening one with the noise of clashing boulders.

THE RIVER TEES AT WYCLIFFE, birthplace of the medieval reforming church-man John Wycliffe who began the first English translation of the Bible.

THE TRANQUILLITY OF A SUMMER DAY by the Tees, probably near Barnard Castle is epitomized in this photograph, again by E. Yeoman. The composition is impeccable, with the two figures lending both a human scale and a focal point to the picture.

IN UPPER TEESDALE ESPECIALLY, summer is an unusual luxury and winter the harsh reality. Both have their beauty. In February 1929 there was a period of intense cold though there was little snow. The waterfall of High Force and the deep pool below it were both completely frozen. The writer remembers being taken as a small boy to see this. The chief impression was one of an unreal silence: the usual roar and tumult of the fall was completely hushed. One was almost afraid to speak and break this awful quiet. This photograph was taken by a photographer of the *Northern Echo* newspaper and appeared in that paper on 19 February 1929.

A TYPICAL WINTER LANDSCAPE in the days before modern snow-clearing machinery. The big snowdrift in the foreground has been laboriously cut through by a gang of men with greased shovels, and the cart tracks show that a vehicle has got through. In the middle distance is Langdon Beck hotel with men and carts outside. In the background is Old Folds farm.

SECTION TWO

Towns and Villages

THE VILLAGE OF STAINDROP with the church tower in the background. Like many south Durham villages, Staindrop is built on two sides of a long and wide green. Staindrop is one of the most attractive villages in Teesdale with a number of fine houses. Its history is closely interwoven with that of Raby and its castle and, until the middle of the nineteenth century, the village was one of the more important in the dale. However, when it was bypassed by the railway it did not develop any further.

TEESDALE HAS ONLY ONE MARKET TOWN, Barnard Castle, a substantial part of which is illustrated by these two photographs taken by E. Yeoman from the vantage point of the tower of St Mary's church. On the left is the broad sweep of the Horse Market and the Market Place with the buttermarket – originally the town hall – in the foreground. An inscription records that the building was erected in 1747 by Thomas Breaks of Barnard Castle. The situation of this building in the middle of the street was complained of as early as 1804 by an anonymous tourist (probably Richard Garland) whose words have been echoed many times since then by coach and lorry drivers. Another anonymous tourist in 1828, however, described it as a 'handsome edifice'. The photograph on the right looks eastward along Newgate and is dominated by the bulk of the Bowes Museum, to the left of which can be seen the army barrack building.

BRIGGATE was one of the older streets in Barnard Castle leading from the town to the river crossing. The buildings on the left of this picture huddled along the foot of the cliff on which the castle stood. Those on the right fronted on to the river and included several eighteenth-century industrial buildings. By the end of the Second World War the area had become cramped and dilapidated, while the narrow road hindered traffic. It was therefore almost completely cleared and rebuilt. Ironically heavy traffic no longer uses the street and the now vanished houses would today have been in great demand for flats and antiques shops. The photograph was probably taken around 1890. Note the pawnbroker's sign on the right.

THE HORSE MARKET AND MARKET PLACE, Barnard Castle, with the church and buttermarket in the background. The unpaved street and cobbled market area are packed with parked carts, traps and other horse-drawn vehicles. The parking problem seems to have been as acute before the First World War as it is now. At least we do not now have the stabling problem which must have existed then.

MOST OF THE VILLAGES in Teesdale sprang up close – but not too close – to the river and, because the river was an important boundary, development was usually restricted to one bank. At Barnard Castle the river crossing was important and the top photograph shows the bridge, the castle ruins and the derelict industrial buildings all blanketed by snow in the severe winter of 1947. At Gainford, on the other hand, there was no need for a bridge but there was a ford and a ferry boat was in use for occasional travellers. The building on the left is the gasworks.

THE VILLAGE OF GAINFORD seen from the church. 'The aspect of the place' wrote Fordyce in his *History of Durham* 'is considered more that of a minor watering place than of a retired village'. 'There is here' he goes on, 'none of that utter poverty and squalid wretchedness which too often meets the eye in the villages of the north'.

GAINFORD was, however, not as pretentious as this sounds. Here is a photograph of a shoemaker's cottage and shop. The rubble walls and sash windows contrast with the more fashionable façades of the neighbouring houses. The upper courses of masonry differ from the rest, suggesting that the pantiled roof was possibly a replacement for an earlier thatched roof of a steeper pitch.

THE WESTERN END of the village of Middleton in Teesdale. The Hude (origin obscure) is the short steep bank leading up to Middleton House, the former headquarters of the London Lead Company. The campanile of the clock tower of this complex, which contained the residence of the superintendent as well as workshops, can be seen in the background. The bridge over the Hudeshope Beck is still known as the Rose & Crown bridge even though the Rose & Crown Inn (out of sight) has been the Working Men's Club for many years. Behind the double-fronted baker's shop was a watermill. The motor car suggests a date around the First World War.

ANOTHER EARLIER PHOTOGRAPH OF MIDDLETON taken before many of the present buildings in the Horse Market were erected in the late nineteenth century. In the background, to the left, the complex of buildings at Middleton House can just be discerned while, on the right, are the Rectory with, in front of it, the church. This is not the present church which was built on the site of its predecessor in 1876. The building on the left is the Talbot Inn.

THE WEST END OF THE VILLAGE OF STAINDROP showing the Wheatsheaf Inn with a brake outside the door. The sign above the door reads 'George Stephenson, ale and spirits, good stabling'. Mr Stephenson was licensee early this century and the owner of this photograph, Mr Hedley, is the present licensee. The photograph clearly shows the wide street and green which help to make Staindrop such an attractive village. Of the nine inns recorded in Staindrop in 1856 three survive.

THE TINY VILLAGE OF LARTINGTON in around 1920. On the left is the village school (now a private house) with its clock tower and playground. In the centre of the picture is one of the thatched houses which formerly were not uncommon in Teesdale. This roof was destroyed by fire around 1920 and replaced by stone slabs. Note the gas street lights and rough surface of the road.

THE WEST END OF THE VILLAGE OF BOWES. The ruins of the castle can be seen on the right. This consisted of a massive stone rectangular keep built in 1187 in the corner of a Roman fort. It was never a residence but a guard tower to watch out for and check Scots raids over Stainmore. Unlike other villages illustrated, Bowes consists of two rows of houses lining a single street which followed the Roman cross-Penine route. Although peaceful enough in this photograph, the road in later years became clogged with a constant stream of cars and heavy lorries effectively splitting the village in two. The recent construction of a bypass has returned the village to its earlier quiet.

THE LITTLE VILLAGE OF HOLWICK which nestles under the whinstone scars. It was here that Richard Watson the poet lived when he wrote his poem 'My Journey to Work' which describes his 14-mile walk each Monday morning to his work in the mines of Little Eggleshope.

A VERY DIFFERENT TYPE OF VILLAGE is found in the northern part of Teesdale, where coal mining was the mainstay of the economy for many years. This is a small part of the village of Butterknowle with the headgear of the Diamond pit in the background. Butterknowle as the name of a village, does not occur in *Whellans Directory* for 1856, although there was a colliery of that name and the whole district of some 6,000 acres had a population of 787. 'There are' says the directory, 'a number of houses built without any regard to regularity . . . chiefly inhabited by agricultural labourers and workmen employed in the neighbouring collieries'. By the time of the 1896 edition the position had changed dramatically, when over 700 men and boys were employed in the mines.

'THE VILLAGE OF COCKFIELD' says Fordyce '. . . is irregularly built and most of its primitive rural character has been superseded by the erection of houses for the colliery population . . .'. One of these groups of houses, on the outskirts of Cockfield at Burnt Houses, is shown here.

SECTION THREE

Buildings

BERNARD'S CASTLE, later Barnard Castle, was begun in the early twelfth century by Bernard Balliol whose father had been given the manor of Gainford by William Rufus. This was part of a policy to control routes across the Pennines and subdue the inhabitants of the hills by building castles at strategic points. Later the town grew up under the protection of the castle. This photograph of the castle under snow by E. Yeoman, shows the strength of its situation and its grandeur even as a ruin.

'SALUTE PROUD RABY'S BATTLED TOWERS' wrote Sir Walter Scott in *Rokeby*. Although much altered in the nineteenth century, Raby remains one of the finest examples, if not the finest, of medieval castle architecture in the north of England. Until the rising of the northern earls in the late sixteenth century it was one of the principal seats of the powerful Neville family, Earls of Westmoreland, who forfeited it to the Crown for the part which they played in the rebellion. In 1626 it was purchased by Sir Henry Vane and has remained with this family since then.

RABY CASTLE REMAINS INTACT, Barnard Castle is a ruin, but Streatlam Castle, pictured here, has been completely destroyed. Its early history is obscure but, in the early-fourteenth century, it passed by marriage to the Bowes family. It was completely rebuilt in the fifteenth century and, a hundred years later, was badly damaged by the rebels during the Rising of the North while its owner Sir George Bowes was defending Barnard Castle. The castle was again completely rebuilt during the eighteenth century and more alterations were made in the nineteenth. By 1939 it had been abandoned by the Bowes family and was taken over by the army who eventually demolished it.

THOUGH MUCH SMALLER THAN THE OTHER CASTLES OF TEESDALE and despite later alterations, Mortham Tower is a fine example of a medieval fortified house. The tower was probably built in the mid-fourteenth century, perhaps after the hamlet of Rokeby had been destroyed by Scots raiders in 1346. Though fortified, the large windows suggest that it was intended primarily as a house rather than a strictly defensive building. Throughout the medieval period it belonged to the Rokeby family who saw much service in the Border wars. In the seventeenth century it was sold, together with Rokeby, to the Robinson family.

ROKEBY HALL is largely the work of Sir Thomas Robinson, described by the *Victoria County History* as 'a typical eighteenth century dilettante and man of fashion.' The estate had been bought from the Rokeby family some years before and Sir Thomas, a gifted amateur architect, rebuilt the house and enclosed the park in 1720–30. He had, however, been too extravagant and was forced to sell the estate to J.S. Morritt, whose son, John Sawrey Morritt, was a classical scholar, traveller and friend of many famous writers and artists.

WEMMERGILL HALL IN LUNEDALE, now derelict, was described in 1856 as 'the favourite shooting box of the Earl of Strathmore'.

THE MOST REMARKABLE BUILDING in Teesdale and indeed one of the most unusual in the county is the Bowes Museum. It was built by John Bowes of Streatlam Castle and his wife Josephine, a French actress, to house their large collections of furniture, pictures, porcelain and many other things. Work on the building, which was designed by a French architect Jules Pellechet, began in 1869. The estimated cost was £38,500 but in fact it cost more than three times this amount. Josephine died in 1874 but the museum was not really completed until after her husband's death in 1885. The official opening took place in 1892. John Bowes' financial affairs had, however, been in turmoil for some time before his death and it was found impossible to open the Museum to the public while legal proceedings went on. It was not until 1909 that the Museum was fully opened. Financial problems continued for many years until, in 1956, the Museum was taken over by Durham County Council. It is now realized that its collections are among the most important in the country. Teesdale is extraordinarily fortunate to possess such a wonderful asset.

THE BOWES MUSEUM UNDER CONSTRUCTION.

THE BOWES MUSEUM ENTRANCE HALL, c. 1930.

THE OLD DURHAM MILITIA BARRACKS in Barnard Castle has now been replaced by housing, although the entrance gate remains intact. The third regiment of militia, later known as the Durham Militia, was raised in 1759, becoming the Durham Light Infantry in 1887. These barracks were built in 1864 and, after falling into disuse, were sold in 1930 to the town of Barnard Castle.

EGGLESTONE ABBEY was founded in the late-twelfth century for Premonstratensian canons and colonized from the existing abbey at Easby near Richmond. Although the buildings were fine and extensive, the abbey was always in financial difficulties. After its suppression in 1540, the abbey was sold to one Robert Strelley who converted the domestic wing into a house. The church and other buildings were used as a source of building stone up until the nineteenth century, while the house eventually became labourers' cottages and then farm buildings. The two photographs show parts of the domestic range as they were in the late nineteenth century before the then Ministry of Works attempted to restore the medieval atmosphere of the site by removing later additions and alterations. Egglestone Abbey is still a popular place for picnics but dancing seems no longer to be a problem.

'THE GRADUAL AND PROGRESSIVE DECAY of more than two centuries has effected the demolition of nearly all but the outward shell of this magnificent fortress [Barnard Castle]. The site is now occupied by an orchard intersected by numerous traces of foundations ... Balliol's tower ... a circular erection of considerable height ... has been kept in better condition than any other part of the castle having been fitted up some years ago as a shot factory ...' Fordyce, *History of Durham*, 1856.

BLAGRAVES HOUSE, named after a previous owner, is the oldest surviving building standing in Barnard Castle. Tradition says that when Oliver Cromwell visited the town he was entertained here. The diary of Wm Sanderson of Egglestone mentions his attendance with other local magistrates at a party to celebrate the accession of King James II. He says, somewhat ruefully, that he spent 20 pounds on this.

'DOTHEBOYS HALL' must be one of the most famous schools which never existed. Charles Dickens' creation of the school in his novel *Nicholas Nickleby* was based on an amalgam of several of the more notorious Yorkshire schools including the one kept by William Shaw in this house in the village of Bowes.

UNLIKE DOTHEBOYS this was not a private academy, but the first National School in Barnard Castle founded in 1814 by subscription and built on the south side of the churchyard. It was demolished in 1896. The government inspector's report on his visit in 1853 included these comments: 'Buildings, a large room, no class-room, a wooden floor has been substituted for a stone one. Eight loose desks. Furniture, clock, stove . . . Books, methods of discipline and instruction, fair . . .' The average attendance at this time was 170. One wonders how they could possibly have been accommodated.

THE OLD CHURCH at Middleton-in-Teesdale. On the left is a most unusual feature – a detached bell-tower – which still survives. The medieval church was not so fortunate; it was demolished, with great difficulty, in 1871 and replaced by the present undistinguished reproduction Gothic building. Presumably the Church of England wished to keep up with the times and to demonstrate that not only Methodists could have new churches.

ANYONE WISHING TO STUDY the gradual development of a typical English parish church should visit Romaldkirk where work of every century can be seen, from the pre-Conquest features in the chancel arch through a fifteenth-century tower to nineteenth-century stained glass. The identity of St Romald was the subject of a long and acrimonious correspondence between the vicars of Romaldkirk, Forest and Staindrop conducted in the *Teesdale Mercury* of 1870. This gradually widened to take in the controversial subject of church restoration continuing with a blast from Staindrop against '... conceited mischievous, meddlesome country parsons who in the sublime audacity of a dense ignorance, sanction ... the destruction of objects they are legally bound to protect ...'. Perhaps not the most tactful of observations.

LIKE ROMALDKIRK, Staindrop is a fine illustration of the evolution of a parish church. It too was an early foundation and includes work of all periods. Perhaps its most notable feature is the number and quality of the Neville family monuments which it contains. The 1896 edition of *Whellan's Directory* says '... the church was restored in 1849 but in spite of the tasteless and destructive manner in which many of the alterations were then carried out, it still remains one of the most interesting ... in the country.'

THE MONASTIC CHRONICLER Symeon of Durham states that in the first half of the ninth century the estate of Gainford (which included Teesdale) with its church was given to the monks of St Cuthbert. The foundation of Gainford church is thus very early and this is confirmed by pre-Conquest sculptured stones found there. The present church was probably begun in the mid-thirteenth century.

THE SMALL CHURCH at Barningham is, in contrast, completely modern, the first church being built in 1816. The photograph shows this church prior to a complete rebuilding in 1891.

THIS CHURCH AT HUTTON MAGNA was completely rebuilt in 1878, although some material from the earlier church was re-used in it. The photograph shows the pre-1878 building.

THE SIMPLE SMALL BUILDING with its unpretentious bell-cote was the parish church at Startforth, dating perhaps from the eleventh or early-twelfth century. It was completely destroyed in 1868 when the present church was built.

THE RUINED THIRTEENTH-CENTURY CHURCH OF ST LAWRENCE at the deserted village of Barforth near Gainford. Since this photograph was taken, probably in the late-nineteenth century, the ruins have considerably diminished. Notice the chimney stack, evidence for the conversion of part of the church into a dwelling for the priest.

THE NEWLY-BUILT WESLEYAN CHAPEL at Middleton-in-Teesdale is seen in the first photograph, while the second shows the same building some years later, after the addition of the manse. The chapel was built in 1870 to hold some 400 people. By the time the second picture was taken the house on the left had also been enlarged. Note the horse and sleigh in the snow.

Tan Hill Inn

—:—

THIS Inn is the highest situated public house in England. It is in the parish of Bowes in North Yorks; about 4 miles from Keld in Swaledale and also about 26½ miles from the historic town of Richmond, Yorks.

The Inn is 1727 feet above the sea level, being 37 feet higher than " The Cat and Fiddle " in Derbyshire.

ON THE EXTREME SOUTHERN EDGE of Teesdale lies Tan Hill, once an area of small coal drift mines but now devoted to sheep, grouse and Pennine Way walkers.

THE BROWN JUG INN at Evenwood Gate probably in the early 1920s. Outside stands the first motor delivery lorry to be used by the brewers, Vaux.

THE NINETEENTH CENTURY had lavished its building skills on chapels and churches while pubs remained, for the most part, little more than good-sized ordinary houses. As the twentieth century progressed the positions were reversed. There were, however, exceptions. The old Stag's Head at the Slack was replaced in 1909, not long after this photograph was taken, by the existing rather ostentatious 'railway Gothic' building. The Black Horse at Ingleton, on the other hand, has remained much the same, though the cottages on the left have long been demolished.

TWO VIEWS OF THE INN AT BOWBANK, Lunedale, which was later a Youth Hostel and is now a farmhouse. Perhaps only 20 years separate these two photographs but they represent two different eras. Not only has the horse been replaced by the motor bike but the house itself has had a 'face-lift'. We can look back on both these with nostalgia, but which would we prefer to live with?

THE LANGDON BECK HOTEL, Forest in Teesdale. The earlier Sportsman's Rest was on the opposite side of the road and was used as farm buildings after the licence was transferred to the new building. It is whitewashed, as are all the houses on the Raby Estate. There are several apocryphal stories about the origin of this practice. When newly whitewashed the farms and buildings look most attractive but, as Tom Sawyer found out, whitewashing is not a pleasant task.

THE ROSE AND CROWN HOTEL, Romaldkirk. The photograph was taken in 1910 and shows the licensee, John Kidd, and his family. Like the inn at Langdon Beck its external appearance has changed very little since then.

THE MORRITT ARMS HOTEL at Greta Bridge. Until the construction of a bypass in 1970, the main A66 road ran past the front of the hotel. By 1929 when this photograph was taken it had become necessary to widen the road. Many Roman finds were made, for the rear of the building abuts a Roman fort. The Morritt Arms is famous for its Dickens connection, as it was here that he made Nicholas Nickleby and Mr Squeers alight on their way to Dotheboys Hall.

THOUGH THIS IS NOT AN OLD PHOTOGRAPH, being taken in the late 1960s, it is perhaps not out of place here. The building which it shows performed two important functions in the village of Newbiggin, the ground floor held the hearse and the upper was the reading room instituted in 1879 and supported by the London Lead Company. The subscription was 6*d.* per month and, as well as newspapers, there was a library of nearly 200 books. It will be seen that though steps lead to the upper room there is neither door nor window. At some time after the demise of lead mining the room apparently became a focus for the youth of the village whose conduct apparently so upset their elders that they closed the building permanently by blocking the door and window.

AGAIN, THIS IS NOT AN OLD PHOTOGRAPH, dating only from 1975, but it shows a building which was an important feature of Barnard Castle for almost 200 years. Ullathornes Mill was built in 1795 providing linen thread for the firm of Ullathorne which supplied every necessity for the business of shoe making to firms in England and France. Until its closure in 1930 the mill was the town's principal employer and, at the height of its success, 3–400 people worked here. Both water and steam power were used. Though the building had various uses during and after the Second World War, it gradually became more and more derelict until its demolition became necessary in 1970.

Balder Mill, Cotherstone.

THIS EVOCATIVE PHOTOGRAPH shows Balder Mill, Cotherstone, one of the many former watermills in Teesdale. Though most of these were corn mills there were also fulling mills and paper mills. It is not often realized how important a role was played by the local corn mill before the advent of the railway made the import of flour possible.

WORKMEN building an extension to the school at Mickleton c. 1906. Like many small village schools it was closed some years ago.

THESE TWO PHOTOGRAPHS show only two of the many features of architectural and historical interest formerly in the buildings of Bridgegate, Barnard Castle. The first-floor window with its pilasters was in the original Co-op store of the town and disappeared in the redevelopment of the 1950s.

THE COAT OF ARMS was more fortunate and survives in the Bowes Museum. It was the sign of one of the craftsmen's guilds of which there were three in Bridgegate. The inscription reads: 'Jeremiah Story 1705, The Lord is All Glorious'. The house later became Barnard Castle's first police station.

SECTION FOUR

Work

THOUGH THIS IS ALSO A RECENT PHOTOGRAPH, taken in the winter of 1963 at Thompson Cottages, Forest of Teesdale, it illustrates the difficulties which the severe winters of the upper dale can still cause, as they did in the past. The milk cans are a reminder of a pattern of farming which, though recent, has now disappeared.

YOUNG NONPAREIL.

1869. 1st prize at Grains o'Beck
1870. 2d ,, Stanhope
1st ,, Middleton Tidale
1st ,, Bowes
2d ,, Egglestone
1st ,, Auey
1st ,, Grains o'Beck
1871. 1st ,, Egglestone
1st ,, Bowes
1st ,, Auey

EGBERT.

1871. 2d prize at Egglestone
1st ,, Bowes
1st ,, Auey
2d ,, Dufton
1872. 2d ,, Middleton Tidale
1st ,, Egglestone and
Silver Cup.

TWO PRIZE-WINNING RAMS with a list of their successes. Their breed is uncertain: they certainly pre-date the development of the Swaledale, which is the most popular hill sheep in the dale today, and somewhat resemble the modern Scots Blackface. A farm diary of 1872 speaks of 'Scotch Premium tups' being bought presumably to improve the native breed and it is possible that these are specimens of such rams. Notice that even in the 1870s sheep were being taken to shows as far apart as Stanhope, Middleton and Dufton (near Appleby).

THE CHANGE IN THE CONFORMATION OF HILL SHEEP is well illustrated by this photograph of Mr A. Bainbridge of Ashdub farm, Ettersgill, with one of his prize-winning rams. The date of the photograph is uncertain but probably c. 1960.

AT MANY PLACES BESIDE UPLAND BECKS the remains of stone-walled sheep pens can still be seen. Occasionally the fragments of a dam can still be identified. These are the traces of a practice long in abeyance: sheep washing. Before summer shearing the sheep were washed to remove sand, soil and peat from their fleece. This made for a better fleece and easier shearing. The dam across the beck would be repaired so that a deep pool was formed, then the sheep were gathered and penned. Often several farms would combine for this. One after another the sheep were caught and pushed or thrown into the pool where they were caught by the washers and thoroughly washed before being allowed to scramble out. It was usually the occasion for a great deal of horseplay and was a favourite entertainment with the children.

THOUGH THE HARDY SWALEDALE SHEEP BECAME DOMINANT in the higher part of the dale, further downhill the Teeswater was developed particularly for crossing with the Swaledale to produce a sheep with better wool and more meat. The characteristics of this breed – its size and long lustrous fleece – are clearly seen in these three show rams photographed in 1914 at Snotterton Hall, Staindrop. Snotterton, incidentally, is a corruption of the Anglo-Saxon 'Cnapaton' which sounds much more attractive.

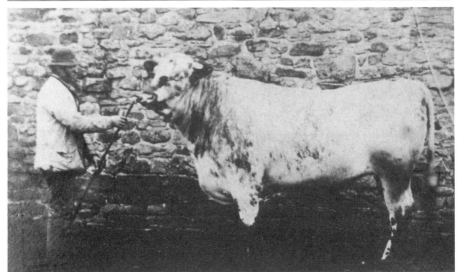

IT WAS IN LOWER TEESDALE that the Shorthorn breed of cattle was developed at the beginning of the nineteenth century. The Shorthorn quickly became by far the most important breed and retained its dominant position until after the Second World War. The reasons for its subsequent rapid decline are too complex for discussion here. Three photographs show different aspects of the breed: first, an early picture of a dales-bred bull, first prizewinner at the first Eggleston Show in 1864; second, Mr J.W. Hodgson of Cotherstone with a typical Shorthorn milk cow c. 1920; and thirdly, a well-known breeder of pedigree cattle of about the same date – Mr Harrison of Gainford with some of his stock, kept more for beef than milk.

HORSES WERE ESSENTIAL FOR FARM WORK of all kinds and their breeding and care was a specialized business. This photograph shows Mr Townson of Hilton Moor Farm (in the background on a grey pony) with two of his farm men (Mr J. Davidson and Mr J. Moses) and three horses. They were returning from a fair in Gainford and are outside the Wheatsheaf Inn at Ingleton. The Wheatsheaf is no longer an inn. Mr Davidson, on the right, worked for Mr Townson and later for his son for 55 years.

IN THE UPPER DALE the heavy work horses seen in the previous picture were replaced by smaller lighter Dales ponies for general farm work. The two haymaking pictures here were both taken at High Green farm, Mickleton, in the 1920s. The boy seated on the horse in the first picture was Tom Dent who also appears with his pet dog in the picture on page 110. The basket in the foreground would have held a picnic tea, perhaps the most popular part of haymaking, especially for the children. Nothing else ever tasted so good. In the second picture the horse rake is being used to 'row-up' the hay in preparation for 'sweeping' it to a shed or stack.

AS WELL AS THE ORDINARY FARM HORSE, faster riding or driving horses were also kept. The photograph shows Mr T. Foster in the yard of the shooting lodge at Wemmergill.

DESPITE HORSES, haymaking required a great deal of hard labour. It was the most important operation of the whole year and getting in the hay took precedence over everything else. Everyone, from the oldest to the youngest, was expected to turn out to help while neighbours and visiting relatives were always sure of a welcome. This is the family at Park End farm, Holwick. The date is uncertain but probably c. 1910.

BUTTERMAKING at West Park, Cotherstone, c. 1915. The making of butter was an important aspect of work on many farms. On the right is the end-over-end churn while, on the left, a butter-worker is being used to remove the buttermilk. Much of the butter produced in Teesdale was taken to the market at Barnard Castle.

TWO MEN AND A BOY building a stone wall by the side of a road between Cotherstone and Romaldkirk. They wear aprons, leggings and clogs. The boy is putting in the 'fillers' of small stones. The pasture in the background shows the terracing of earlier ploughing. The technique of building a stone wall depends on the constraints imposed by the material: here a well-bedded sandstone is being used which is an ideal walling stone. Note the two layers of large slabs known as 'throughs' which bind the wall together.

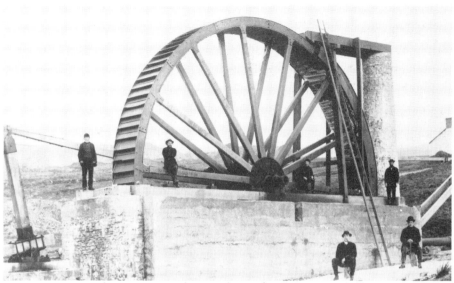

MOST LEADMINES made ingenious and inspired use of waterpower to drive their machinery. Many were situated in remote situations where no other power source was practicable. In any case water was plentiful, free and reusable. This large over-shot wheel was at Greenhurth mine and is shown just after its installation. It was situated as low as possible to reuse water from higher ore-dressing floors. Power from the wheel was transmitted by a system of rods and spears to a shaft 500 yards away. Alas, none of the many wheels remains.

IN THE LATE-EIGHTEENTH CENTURY the London Lead Company made Middleton its headquarters for operations in the north of England, building a large house for the resident superintendent with, at the rear, extensive workshops. These employed joiners, masons, blacksmiths, millwrights and other tradesmen so that all necessary maintenance work on the company's mines could be carried out by their own workmen.

AS WELL AS MINING THE LEAD ORE the London Lead Company processed it at one or other of their smelt mills, producing not only lead but also silver. This photograph, taken perhaps in the 1920s, shows the ruins of the smelt mill at Copley. Though individual buildings cannot be identified, it is evident that this was a large and complex site.

THE CHIMNEY OF THE COPLEY SMELT MILL which is the last surviving smelt mill chimney in the area. These tall chimneys were built at the end of a long covered flue and were usually some distance from the mill itself. This gave a greater draught, helped disperse the poisonous fumes and made it possible for the lead dust, which used to accumulate in the flue, to be removed later.

THERE WAS ALSO AN IMPORTANT SMELT MILL at Blackton near Egglestone though very little of it now remains. In his poem 'My Journey to Work', Richard Watson the lead-miner poet wrote:

A vapour dense ascents on yonder hill
From the smelting works of Blackton mill;
Long may it rise in curling wreaths on high
And ore be raised each furnace to supply
To give employment to the neighbouring poor
And keep the wolf named 'want' far from their door.

DESPITE RICHARD WATSON'S HOPES the smelt mill did eventually close after the collapse of the whole leadmining industry. In 1932 the chimney too was demolished by Tom Allinson of Egglestone, one of the last of the lead-miners. A large crowd gathered to watch and cheered heartily when the job was completed. We may regret the destruction, but most acknowledge that it was a symbol of the end of the bad old days of poverty and pollution.

AS WELL AS LEAD there were also thin seams of coal at some places higher on the fells. These had been worked in a small desultory way since Roman times but in only a few places were they commercially viable. One of these areas was Tan Hill, on the border with Swaledale, where small drift mines were producing coal at least at the beginning of the nineteenth century. These two photographs were probably taken c. 1930.

ONE OF THE FEW PHOTOGRAPHS of underground workings. This mine gallery is quite spacious, though the roof timbers look none too safe. Its provenance is not certain but it is probably one of the drift mines in the north-east part of Teesdale where, during the second half of the nineteenth century, coal mining became the major industry.

A GROUP OF MINERS WITH A TUB. The man on the right has obviously been working underground. Note the two boys in the picture who both seem very young. A report of 1894 commented '... we are glad to perceive that a serious attempt is about to be made to ameliorate the condition of these juvenile white slaves ... the 'trapper' may begin work in his twelfth year ... his duties are to open and shut the doors as the trucks pass and repass ... his shelter is a damp dark recess, his working day is ten hours and his average pay is rather less than a shilling a day ...'. Even so, he was better paid than the washer boys of the lead industry whose wage was 4*d*. – 6*d*. a day.

A GROUP OF MINERS AT RANDOLPH COLLIERY, Evenwood. They carry lamps and walking sticks and are presumably about to start a shift.

IN CONTRAST TO THE UPPER PICTURE, this shows the officials of the Woodland and Crake Scar collieries in 1913. It is interesting to note that they were all men of experience averaging 23 years service each.

A GROUP OF BOYS AND THEIR PIT PONIES at one of the drift mines on Railey Fell, Ramshaw. The photograph was probably taken in the early 1920s. The mine closed in 1939. The report of 1894 quoted above went on: '... at fifteen years of age as a minimum the boy miner may become a *driver* ... the calls upon him may now be incessant during the whole of his ten hours, at times he may have breathing spaces and brief periods of comparative leisure but his duties are both onerous and responsible and his wages are about 1s. 4d. per day ...'.

RANDOLPH COLLIERY, Evenwood, showing the winding gear, incline and rail network.

MUCH OF THE COAL from Randolph Colliery was used to produce coke. The coking plant was built in 1895 and extended in 1897. In 1909 the batch of 50 patent by-product ovens shown here was built. The next major improvement to the works did not take place until 1947. The coke works were closed and demolished in 1984.

THE CHIMNEY OF THE DIAMOND PIT, Butterknowle, being repaired by a local builder, Mr G. Howey, with his son and brother and, of course, a dog. Obviously the photograph was taken long before the advent of Health and Safety at Work regulations, for the ladder stands on a platform supported by bricks which in turn rest on balks of timber resting on top of barrels. Nevertheless the repairs were carried out satisfactorily.

BOTH LEADMINING AND COALMINING were dangerous and unhealthy occupations. Tuberculosis, silicosis and other lung complaints were ubiquitous. A glance through the nineteenth-century census returns shows very few retired miners! This photograph shows a group of coal miners at a Convalescent Home at Grange over Sands, c. 1930.

AS WELL AS LEAD AND COALMINING, quarrying has been an important industry in Teesdale. Though large-scale quarrying only began after the arrival of the railway, limestone and freestone has always been worked on a small scale and at many locations. These smaller quarries continued to be used intermittently whenever there was a demand for their product and, in recent years, there has been a revival in their fortunes, with several quarries operating full time and producing large quantities of stone. This photograph shows a small quarry at Cotherstone, probably during the 1920s though the horse and cart and small windlass would have changed little over the preceding hundred years.

NO EARLY PHOTOGRAPH has so far come to light showing the making of the stone roof-slabs so characteristic of Teesdale houses. This recent photograph shows Mr H. Cross and an assistant at Shipley quarry making roof-slabs in the traditional manner. The slab on the right has been marked out and is being cut to size. On the left, Mr Cross is making a hole for fixing the slab in place.

THE QUARTZ DOLERITE of the Great Whin Sill, which outcrops in spectacular fashion at many places in Upper Teesdale, is a very hard rock and was found to be eminently suitable for making paving 'sets' for city streets. These were made by hand to a standard size. The photograph shows the production of the rough blocks from which the sets were chipped to shape. As with other quarry products it was only the arrival of the railway which made the production and distribution of these 'sets' possible.

A VERY DIFFERENT QUARRY SCENE is shown here in 1907 in Lunedale. Six people – surely three sisters and their husbands? – in their best clothes stand in the 'kebble', an iron bucket used to lift loads of stone. Another lady prepares to photograph the scene while a very apprehensive lady and gentleman look on. Perhaps they are not too confident of the strength of the wire rope?

ORD AND MADDISON'S 60 workers at the whinstone quarry at Middleton in Teesdale before the First World War. Note how many boys were employed in what was a hard and dangerous environment. The man on the right, Mr Gowland, was at that time clerk at the quarry. He appears among the group of cyclists on page 120 and again on page 94 after he had left the quarry and started a motor business.

THORNGATE FACTORY, Barnard Castle, seen from the south bank of the river. This was a woollen mill and, unlike most of the others in the town, was powered by steam from the beginning. The chimney was demolished in 1933 but the factory premises continued to be used until recently, making protective clothing. In 1986 the building was acquired by Teesdale Building Preservation Trust and converted into flats.

DUNN'S CARPET FACTORY, Bridgegate, Barnard Castle, before its demolition after the Second World War. Carpet weaving seems to have begun in Barnard Castle by the early part of the nineteenth century and, by the middle of the century, was the chief industry of the town though it began to decline soon after that.

AS WELL AS THE MAJOR INDUSTRIES of mining, quarrying and textiles, Teesdale had its share of the usual rural craft trades, of which this photograph may serve as an example. It shows Mr Parmley, joiner, outside his workshop at Middleton with a cart which he had just finished building. The photograph was probably taken just before the First World War.

DURING THE FIRST WORLD WAR home-grown timber had to replace imports and many woods were felled. This photograph shows a team of horses with a load of logs at Cotherstone.

ROADWORKS ON GRANT BANK, Gainford, c. 1930. Drains are being laid and this Leyland tipper seems to be dumping backfill.

ALTHOUGH ROCHDALE is usually credited with being the birthplace of the Co-operative movement, Middleton should really have that honour. In January 1842 a group of miners, with help from their employers, The London Lead Company, formed the 'Governor and Company's Teesdale Workmen's Corn Association' in order to provide flour at a cheaper price than that charged by local millers. After a shaky start the venture prospered. In 1873 the name of the society was changed to 'The Teesdale Workmen's Industrial and Provident Society' and a grocery shop was opened. The photograph shows the staff outside later premises which were destroyed by fire in 1929.

THE CO-OPERATIVE MOVEMENT flourished in Teesdale during the nineteenth century. This photograph shows the Butterknowle branch shortly after its opening in 1896. It closed some years ago and has recently been demolished.

THE BUTCHER'S CART CALLS. The date and exact location of this photograph are unknown. It is often forgotten that, in the days before bus services and private cars, people in rural areas were well served by travelling tradesmen – butcher, greengrocer and grocer all called at least once a week and often there was fierce competition between different shops. Notice the large joints displayed as well as pigs' heads and the basket of sausages.

THIS PHOTOGRAPH OF THE STAFF OF BARNARD CASTLE POST OFFICE was presented to the Postmistress, Miss Monkhouse (centre) on her retirement in 1902. The old post office was on the west side of the Bank.

BARNARD CASTLE FIRE BRIGADE. Date and place unfortunately are not known.

BEFORE THE MECHANIZED SNOW CLEARING which today ensures that roads remain open for all but a few days in the most severe winters, most farms and villages expected to be snowbound for days and weeks at a time. Horse-drawn wooden ploughs cleared the roads when the snow was not too deep, but drifts had to be dug out by hand. Where the snow was very deep this entailed two or three 'lifts'. The gangs of men, usually composed of the unemployed, had to walk to their work and all too often after a hard day would find that overnight snow and wind meant that they had to start all over again.

FROM THE LATTER PART OF THE NINETEENTH CENTURY the growth of industry and population on Teesside led to a greatly increased demand for water and a programme of reservoir building on the tributaries of the Tees was begun. The first of these reservoirs were at Blackton and Hury in Baldersdale. The upper photograph shows the puddle trench of the Blackton reservoir under construction in June 1892. Note the rail-mounted crane and the steam roller. The lower photograph shows the excavation of the flood water channel at the same reservoir also in 1892. A huge steam 'navvy' tips its load into horse-drawn tubs travelling on rails.

THE RESERVOIR CONSTRUCTION used huge quantities of rubble and dressed stone. Quarries were opened to produce it and railway lines built to transport it to the site. Here is the scene at Catty Crag quarry.

ONE OF THE DIFFICULTIES of building a reservoir on a fast flowing river liable to sudden floods is illustrated by this photograph of the toe of the bye wash at Hury reservoir. This had been spanned by a footbridge which was washed away by a flood in September 1891 leaving only the abutments.

SECTION FIVE

Road and Rail

THE UNMETALLED NARROW TRACK seen here is now the busy dual-carriageway A66 trunk road across Stainmore. The stump of stone is the remains of the Rey Cross, originally an Anglo-Scandinavian cross built beside the Roman road and possibly commemorating the death nearby of Erik Bloodaxe in 954. For several hundred years thereafter it marked the boundary between Northumbria and Cumbria and since Cumbria was normally under Scots control the effective boundary between England and Scotland.

A GROUP OF CARRIERS on the road above High Force in 1912. They are returning to Cow Green mine. Up to the middle of the nineteenth century most of the carriage of lead was done by pack ponies known as 'jaggers' but improved roads thereafter meant that horses and carts could be used. The carts were usually small because of the weight of lead ore and its accompanying minerals.

THOUGH THIS PHOTOGRAPH IS OF APPROXIMATELY THE SAME DATE it is of a very different equipage. Mr Arthur Watson of Aukside, Middleton, is driving his locally famous Dales pony stallion 'Teesdale Comet'.

The Posting Houses, Middleton-in-Teesdale.

THE TITLE ON THIS POSTCARD 'THE POSTING HOUSES, MIDDLETON' refers to the two inns. The one on the left was the Blue Bell, now no longer licenced, while that in the centre of the picture was the Cleveland Arms. It was formerly known as the Cross Keys but was renamed after extensive alterations around 1890. The photograph was probably taken at this time. Notice the plaque of the Cyclists Touring Club above the archway. The building on the right is now Barclay's Bank. The coaches would travel from the railway terminus at Middleton.

IN THE DAYS BEFORE MOTOR TRANSPORT when the horse was king, the blacksmith's shop was perhaps the most important tradesman's premises. Even the smallest village had its blacksmith. His shop was also the accepted meeting place for the men and boys of the village; there was a fire, always something happening, a chance to meet strangers and an opportunity for gossip. The upper picture shows the blacksmith's shop at Mickleton and the lower, the shop at Whorlton.

CARTS AND SLEDGES IN THE SNOW outside Langdon Beck Hotel. Almost certainly they are waiting to collect the monthly provisions which will, in bad weather, be left at the hotel by the Co-op delivery cart. Sledges were used extensively on Teesdale farms until the Second World War and not just during winter. Where roads were non-existent a horse-drawn sledge could travel where a wheeled vehicle could not go.

MR TOM IRELAND, THE POSTMAN, on his rounds in the upper dale with pony and sledge.

THE FIRST WORLD WAR showed the value of motor transport and in many places after the war garages were opened and cars, lorries and charabancs made their appearance. The first picture shows Gowland's garage at Middleton, Mr Gowland (who appears on page 70 as clerk at a quarry) is on the left. Mr H.L. Beadle who kindly lent this photograph is the central figure. There are three Peerless lorries, an International, a Fiat, a Maudsley and a Daimler. The second photograph of three cars was taken at the same garage.

TWO EARLY COACHES. The upper one shows the first bus service in Evenwood run by Emmerson and Rycroft. The occasion of the outing is not known but there seems to be a little mechanical problem. The owner of the vehicle in the lower picture is Mr Fred Lowe of Middleton who leans on the front mudguard. His son Clarry is at the wheel. Whether the group of youngsters were going anywhere or were just posing for their picture is debatable.

WHILE MOST PEOPLE who at the end of the war were interested in motor cars were content to buy and operate them, one group decided to make them. A small company was set up in Barnard Castle to produce the Black Prince cycle car. Two models were made, one with a single cylinder engine and the other with a twin. The engine was air cooled and the cars were belt driven. Despite enthusiastic reports in the local press the company was soon in financial difficulties and ceased production. So far as is known only one – much restored – specimen of the cars has survived. This was recently acquired by the Bowes Museum where it is now on display.

AFTER THE SUCCESS OF THE DARLINGTON TO STOCKTON RAILWAY there were several attempts to obtain parliamentary approval for a line to Barnard Castle. There were, however, many objections from trustees of the turnpike roads and from landowners so that it was not until 1854 that an Act received royal assent and work could begin. The estimated cost for the construction was £7,000 per mile. It is difficult to exaggerate the changes to the economy of Teesdale brought about by the arrival of the railway. It is, however, easy to forget the immense effort which was needed for such projects to be successful: many aspects of construction required new and relatively untried technology. In this photograph a cutting is being made near Barnard Castle.

THE ARRIVAL OF RAIL led to a great expansion in the production of coal which could now be easily distributed and spur lines were built to all collieries. This locomotive, *Nelson*, was built in 1871 by Kitson of Leeds and used to haul coal from Woodland colliery between 1885 and 1922. After the closure of the colliery the engine was used on a reservoir construction project in South Wales.

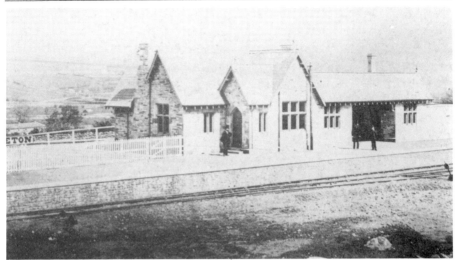

NO SOONER HAD THE DARLINGTON–BARNARD CASTLE LINE BEEN OPENED than plans were made for an extension to Middleton: '. . . it will be of great advantage in conveying cattle from the west to the great consuming districts of the iron fields . . . and facilitate the transmission of grain to the grazing districts . . . (it will) open out to tourists the splendid scenery of Teesdale as well as the mineral resources of that lovely dale . . .'. The photograph of Middleton station, shortly after its opening in 1868, was taken by Jacob Readshaw (see page 104) quite possibly with a camera made by himself. The station is now a caravan site.

THIS ATTRACTIVE CHRISTMAS CARD shows the little station at Bowes on the cross-Pennine route between Barnard Castle and Tebay. The line was completed in 1861 and was, for most of its life, an important freight line, carrying in particular coke from the Durham coalfield to Cumberland and Lancashire and iron ore in return. The date of the card is not certain but is probably around 1910.

EVENWOOD STATION on the line between Bishop Auckland and Barnard Castle. It was built in 1884 succeeding an earlier station.

THREE VIEWS OF BARNARD CASTLE STATION, c. 1935. The Darlington–Barnard Castle railway was opened in 1856 after a long battle between rival proponents of schemes and also the major landowners and turnpike trustees. The original station was later used as a goods station. The new passenger station was built in 1861 at the junction of the line with the Barnard Castle–Tebay line. In 1863 the Barnard Castle–Bishop Auckland line was opened and in 1869 the line was extended to Middleton. Barnard Castle thus became a very busy station and junction. It closed completely in 1965.

AMONG THE PROBLEMS FACED BY THE EARLY RAILWAY BUILDERS was that of crossing the many deep valleys. The two photographs here are of viaducts across the Tees (above) and the Deepdale Beck (below). Both were designed by Thomas Bouch; that across the Tees on stone piers and that across Deepdale entirely of iron. It is a remarkable tribute to the skills of the engineer and builders that both lasted for over 100 years carrying loads far in excess of those for which they were designed. Both, sadly, were demolished in the 1970s. Another even bigger viaduct on the Stainmore line was also built by Bouch and was the occasion for a long poem by J. Close the station master of Kirby Stephen.

THE EARLY RAILWAYS in Teesdale were all single track, but the volume of coal traffic in particular soon led to the doubling of much of the track. The photograph shows Lands viaduct being widened in 1904/5.

THE GREAT RAILWAY VIADUCTS were, of course, only a modern manifestation of a very old tradition of bridge building and it is interesting to note that while the viaducts had only a relatively brief life span many of Teesdale's bridges have a long history. This beautiful arch, photographed in the early years of the century, stands just as it has done since it was built in the fourteenth century. It is at Barforth (see page 41).

THIS SMALL PACK-HORSE BRIDGE crosses Thorsgill Beck beside Egglestone Abbey. It is now partly hidden by the road bridge which has replaced the ford shown here.

BARNARD CASTLE BRIDGE, now fortunately closed to heavy traffic, has a long history. Though the Roman road between Bowes and Binchester crossed the river here, there is no evidence of a Roman bridge. The present bridge is of two arches, one higher than the other, however, Leland in the sixteenth century describes it as having three arches. It is possible that it was badly damaged during the seige of the castle in 1569 and had to be rebuilt. An inscription 'ER 1569' on a stone in the north wall is a replacement for one described in 1856 as being nearly illegible. Whatever may have happened in earlier years, the bridge was certainly badly damaged in the great flood of 1771 although it was one of the few bridges in the North to remain standing. It is said that in the seventeenth century one Cuthbert Hilton used to celebrate illegal marriages in the centre of the bridge.

RUTHERFORD BRIDGE, on the road from Barnard Castle to Scargill, was built in 1773 in place of a seventeenth-century bridge which crossed the Greta at this point. Its name perpetuates the name of a medieval village now lost.

GILMONBY BRIDGE, BOWES, also across the river Greta, connects the two villages of Bowes and Gilmonby.

CERTAINLY THE BEST KNOWN BRIDGE IN TEESDALE and one of the best known in England is this at Greta Bridge which has been a favourite subject for generations of artists. Perhaps the best known picture is that by Cotman. There may have been a Roman bridge on the site, for the Roman fort is only a few yards away. The bridge was built by Mr Morritt in 1773 at a cost of £850. When looking at its graceful arch and slender balustraded parapet it is difficult to imagine that, until 1970 when a bypass was begun, it carried the constant stream of heavy lorries and cars travelling on the main cross-Pennine road.

IT IS SOMEWHAT IRONIC that this slender bridge, the Abbey bridge at Barnard Castle, must now carry the heavy traffic between the town and the A66 trunk road. It is a beautiful bridge of one arch high above the gorge through which the Tees runs. As the photograph shows it was, for many years, a toll bridge with rooms for the keeper at the Yorkshire end. These unfortunately have been demolished and only the foundations remain.

WINCH BRIDGE which spans the Tees near the hamlet of Bowlees. The present bridge is the latest of several suspension bridges to have been built at this place. The first, using wrought iron chains, was built by lead-miners living at Holwick to enable them to cross the river on their way to work. William Hutchinson in his *History of Durham*, Vol III, 1794, describes it as '... seventy feet in length and little more than two feet broad with a handrail on one side and planked in such a manner that the traveller experiences all the tremulous motion of the chain and sees himself suspended over a roaring gulph ...'. In 1802 a man fell off this bridge and was drowned while, in 1820, there was another fatality when the bridge chains broke.

THIS FOOTBRIDGE ACROSS THE TEES AT MIDDLETON in 1869 was built – as the name Step Ends tells us – as an alternative to the stepping stones which must often have been impossible to use. The bridge had been built to give access to the station for people living in the lower part of Middleton and was much used. The great flood of 1881, however, proved too much for it and it was carried away. Unlike most of the other bridges damaged by this flood it was not replaced.

ANOTHER CASUALTY of the 1881 flood was this footbridge crossing the river at the bottom of Thorngate in Barnard Castle. This flood on 9 March was the result of heavy snow on 4, 5 and 6 March followed by a sudden thaw, '. . . precisely at twelve minutes to twelve o'clock loud above the deafening roar of the seething water a crack was heard. The bridge literally parted in the centre, rolled over and was swept away . . . two men on the Durham side of the bridge were swept away . . .'. This bridge was replaced by the present one.

NOT THE FAMOUS PHOTOGRAPH OF THE TACOMA NARROWS BRIDGE, USA, but the collapse of the footbridge at Cotherstone in 1929.

THERE WERE OTHER RISKS TO TRAVELLERS besides collapsing bridges. We often forget the accidents which beset both rail and road travel. This photograph shows the results of a head on collision between two NER engines near Gainford in 1905.

IT HAS NOT YET BEEN POSSIBLE to trace the date or exact place where this car came to a decided halt on the Stainmore road.

SECTION SIX

People

A GROUP OF CRAFTSMEN — mechanics at Woodland colliery. Note how all age groups are represented in the photograph and how the individuality of each of these very different men comes through despite the rather formal pose.

THIS GROUP having their 'bait' in the culvert of Hury reservoir in 1892 are not craftsmen but some of the many labourers employed. The man in the centre of the picture was known as 'Long Charlie' and was obviously one of the best known characters on the site.

CONTRASTING WITH THE PICTURE ABOVE is this group of engineers, surveyors and foremen employed on the same reservoir construction programme. The two foremen, wearing the traditional bowler, were brothers.

MOST OF THE EARLY PORTRAIT PHOTOGRAPHS were studio pictures and Teesdale had several excellent photographers. Probably the best was E. Yeoman who worked in Barnard Castle and many of whose photographs are reproduced in this book. This portrait of Miss Annie Allinson is characteristic of his painstaking work.

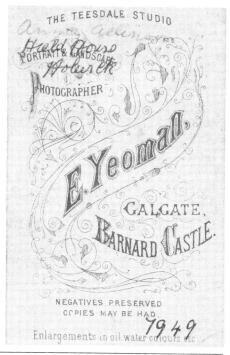

ON THESE TWO PAGES we see the photographs of the most influential people in Teesdale in
the late-nineteenth century. As well as his Scottish estates, the Earl of Strathmore, seen here
with his countess on the terrace at Streatlam Castle, owned much of Teesdale south of the
river and west of Barnard Castle. The Teesdale estates of the Duke of Cleveland (above)
were even more extensive, stretching along the north bank of the river from Piercebridge to
the head of the dale (though there were, of course, enclaves under other ownership). A
common saying in Teesdale was to the effect that only two things were certain: death and
the duke's rent day and that the second was the more urgent of the two. Rent days and the
general administration of the estate was in the hands of the head agent Mr Scarth (bottom,
right) seen here at work in the office at Middleton.

ONE OF THE FEW KNOWN PORTRAITS OF RICHARD WATSON, poet and lead-miner. He was born in Middleton in 1833 the son of a lead-miner and, as a child, showed a talent for writing verse. Most of his working life was spent in the mines, although he tended to neglect his employment in favour of writing and published a book of collected verse. An accident in 1891 led to the amputation of a foot, later that year he was sent to Edinburgh for treatment where he died in October after writing his epitaph.

... a poor hardworking rustic bard
his lot indeed was crooked and hard
of comforts wealth bestows; debarred:
a load of woes
to suffering worth 'tis the reward
this world bestows ...

IN 1870 THE *TEESDALE MERCURY* CARRIED A BRIEF REPORT that Jacob Readshaw of Roseberry Cottage, Middleton, had constructed a 6 ft reflecting telescope. He was a man of great ingenuity and craftsmanship: cabinet-maker, wood-carver, photographer, painter and, as we can see here, amateur astronomer.

MR J. INGRAM DAWSON, born in 1862, came from a Westmorland family but went to school at Gainford and, after qualifying as a solicitor, practiced in Barnard Castle for many years and held several public offices in the town. His brief autobiography, *Reminiscences of a Rascally Lawyer* published in 1949, is a mine of information about Teesdale during his life time. As a solicitor, a profession which he never liked, he was well-known for his defence of people prosecuted for poaching offences.

WILLIAM BURNEY OF MICKLETON, shoemaker and poacher pictured wearing the uniform of the Teesdale Rifle Volunteers. It is quite possible that he was one of the men defended by Mr Dawson!

A VERY EARLY PHOTOGRAPH of the author's great-grandfather Thomas Horn Thompson (b.1819), leadminer and smallholder, with his wife, taken in a Penrith studio.

A FINE PORTRAIT from the collection of the late Altred Nevison of Barnard Castle. Mr Kirtley, shown here at his work bench, was a wood-turner in the town. The photograph was exhibited and won prizes at Glasgow and Stirling in 1912.

A PORTRAIT OF EDWARD SMITH who was reputed to be the original on whom Dickens based his character Smike in *Nicholas Nickleby*. Mr Smith became a miner, gardener and ostler in the Lynesack district and was buried in the churchyard there.

MR ANTHONY CLARKE who was the town crier and bellman of Barnard Castle for many years. The photograph was probably taken in the early 1920s.

THIS IMPRESSIVE BEARDED FIGURE is that of Frank Shields who installed himself as a hermit, first at Egglestone Abbey and later at the castle where he acted as unofficial custodian and guide. It is said that he was eventually evicted because of his habit of frightening late passers-by by suddenly appearing in a white sheet! The photograph must date from just after 1850.

ONE OF THE BEST KNOWN MEN IN UPPER TEESDALE between the wars was Mr Fred Thompson, seen here on the Alston road at Middleton with the Co-op delivery cart. Born in 1888, he started work for the Co-op not long after leaving school and, after a spell in the shop, became their delivery man responsible for taking the monthly order of flour, groceries and cattle feed to farms and cottages of the dale. This meant long days in all kinds of weather for, particularly in winter, the non-arrival of the cart would have been a serious matter. Eventually the horse and cart were replaced by a lorry which he continued to drive until his retirement.

A COALMINER FROM ESSEX ROW, Butterknowle, in his working gear: clogs, heavy three-quarter length trousers, waistcoat and jacket, neckerchief and cap. He carries his lamp round his neck, slung over his shoulder in his 'bait' tin with his dinner and a bottle, probably of tea, in his jacket. Essex Row was so called because it housed a number of families who had moved from Essex to find work.

TOM DENT OF HIGH GREEN, MICKLETON, with his pet dog harnessed to a small soap-box cart. He is obviously enjoying it but the dog does not seem too sure. The same boy can be seen in the upper photograph on page 56.

THREE SOLEMN LITTLE GIRLS outside their front door in Evenwood.

PHOTOGRAPHS OF SCHOOLS WITH STAFF AND CHILDREN are among the most common of old photographs. Here is Mr Garrett, schoolmaster at Romaldkirk.

THE STAFF OF GAINFORD ACADEMY in 1876. The seated man, just to the left of centre, is Mr Tennick the art master whose paintings and drawings of local scenes are much prized today. One pupil of the school who later achieved fame was Stan Laurel the comedian.

TWO PHOTOGRAPHS OF THE VILLAGE SCHOOL at Newbiggin which has been closed for many years. The first was probably taken around 1865–70, when the population of the upper dale was at its height. The number on the roll was 60 in 1857 and by 1870 it had increased to 127 – far more than the building could accommodate. The lower photograph shows the schoolchildren in 1936. By 1939 the roll had fallen to 38.

SCENES INSIDE A SCHOOL ARE NOT SO COMMON. This is Woodland School on what must have been a special occasion, for the children are all wearing their best clothes. The class seems to have been modelling trees in Plasticine or some similar material, while the walls are decorated with their pictures of leaves and flowers. Small village schools like this usually made good use of their environment and most children probably knew more about the birds, plants and insects of the area than they do today.

EGGLESTONE SCHOOLCHILDREN on the road outside the Three Tuns Inn. Unfortunately the date and occasion of this photograph are unknown.

THE NATIONAL SCHOOL AT BARNARD CASTLE is shown on page 37. This photograph shows the headmaster, Mr J.J. Bailey (centre), with his former pupil-teachers at Egglestone Abbey in 1864, the 50th anniversary of the opening of the school.

PHOTOGRAPHS OF FAMILIES AT HOME ARE NOT SO COMMON. This charming picture taken at East Loups farm, Cotherstone, (now largely destroyed) shows the truly family nature of dales farming, with everyone, even the smallest, helping.

THE HODGSON FAMILY outside their home in Cotherstone. The rather sombre mood is a reflection of the occasion; two sons are returning to their units in the First World War.

THREE PHOTOGRAPHS OF THE EDLESTON FAMILY of Gainford. First, Revd Edleston, vicar of Gainford, in his garden with, below, the family playing croquet on the lawn and, opposite, with their coach on Winston Bridge.

GILMONBY HALL, BOWES, home of the Headlam family as it was in 1872. The Rt Hon. T.E. Headlam and his wife are beside the ornamental lake. House, gardens and lake have all gone.

A CAREFULLY POSED PHOTOGRAPH of members of the Headlam family at Gilmonby Hall around 1872. The photographer is unknown, but the quality of composition argues for a professional of artistic ability.

THE STAFF OF GILMONBY HALL. Though a clear and factual record, there is no attempt at the sort of composition seen in the upper photograph.

SECTION SEVEN

Leisure

A PHOTOGRAPHERS OUTING by the Tees at Cotherstone in 1905. It would be interesting to know what happened to the photographs taken by the other members of the group.

THREE YOUNG MIDDLETON MEN relaxing carelessly beside their cycles. Their moustaches, pipes and knickerbockers help to give a desired impression of fashionable sportsmen. The man in the centre, Mr Gowland, can also be seen on page 70 and page 84.

CYCLING WAS A SPORT which soon became quite highly organized with clubs and competitions flourishing. Here we see the members of the Barnard Castle Cyclists Meet Committee together with two very young recruits.

THE BARNARD CASTLE EXCELSIOR CYCLING CLUB wearing their club ties and boaters. Their president Mr (later Lt.-Col.) W. Watson is in the centre. The man on the extreme right holds an early petrol-engined cycle. Was this allowed?

AN EVEN MORE ENERGETIC SPORT. Here are the members of the Barnard Castle harriers with the prizes which they won in the 1885 season. The watches, clocks, glassware and cases of cutlery show that they were very successful.

THE MEMBERS OF WHAM CRICKET CLUB in 1915. Though football was the more popular game, most villages could and did field a cricket team, though only a few players could afford the white flannels and the state of the wicket could usually be described as 'unpredictable'.

THE CUP WINNING COPELAND ALBION FOOTBALL TEAM of 1932/33. All the players came from the one street of Copeland Row.

BARNARD CASTLE BOWLS CLUB outside the pavilion in the grounds of the Bowes Museum. The caption reads 'A. Winpenny wins presidents gold medal, Sept. 19 1912'. In the background is the unfinished, and later demolished, Catholic church.

THE MEMBERS OF MIDDLETON GOLF CLUB in 1914. A golf course was begun on the rough pasture overlooking the station but became a casualty of the war and was never revived.

THERE WERE, OF COURSE, OTHER GAMES AND SPORTS. One of the most popular was quoits which required little in the way of facilities or equipment and has seen a revival in recent years. The player pictured here was Mr J. Bates, landlord of the Stags Head Inn, Butterknowle, 1908–1921.

SKATING WAS A MUCH MORE POPULAR SPORT in the severe winters of the nineteenth century though rarely practiced today. While ponds are regularly frozen it is rare for the river ice to be firm enough for skating as it was here in 1929.

A GROUP OF MINERS AND A FEW CHILDREN with their dogs outside the Black Swan Inn, Wham, c. 1915. The two pugilists are posing for the photographer: if it had been a real fight the spectators would have been watching the action and not the camera.

VARIANTS OF THIS GAME OF KNUR AND SPEL, known locally as 'buckstick' are known from all over the north. A small wooden ball – later a golf ball was used – carved by the owner from a hard wood like holly, was placed in a cup on a spring held down by a catch (the knur). The player was armed with a buckstick (the spel): a block of hard wood spliced to the end of a tough and springy shaft such as ash or hickory. With this he released the catch and, as the ball was flung in the air, tried to hit it as far as possible. This is not easy and requires a good eye and quick reflexes. There was much gambling on the distances achieved and some arguments over the ownership of a particular ball. It was also an advantage to have a number of small boys to return the balls!

A MEET OF THE TEES VALLEY BEAGLES at Romaldkirk, C. 1930.

A PIGEON-SHOOTING MATCH at Holwick in 1912. Nowadays of course 'clay pigeons' are used as targets, being flung into the air by a spring but, as this picture shows, originally live pigeons were used.

BRASS BAND MUSIC was extremely popular in all the Dales in the nineteenth and early-twentieth centuries. Almost every village had its band and these were much in demand to play at carnivals, agricultural shows and other functions. The group shown here was from Woodland.

BARNARD CASTLE OPERATIC AND DRAMATIC SOCIETY was for many years an important feature of the town's leisure life. Here is the cast of their production of *Trial by Jury* just before the start of the first performance.

THE BOY SCOUT MOVEMENT was well supported in Teesdale, especially between the wars, when it was greatly encouraged by the then Lord Barnard. This, much earlier, photograph shows the Woodland troop on parade.

A VERY DIFFERENT ORGANIZATION was the junior section of the Good Templars, a temperance society very active in the early years of the century. This was the Evenwood branch.

SECTION EIGHT

Occasions

Romaldkirk Fair 3.

THE PRINCIPAL VILLAGES IN TEESDALE all held fairs at traditionally set dates in the year. These have all long been abandoned though their places have in some instances been filled with agricultural shows. The photograph is of the sheep pens at Romaldkirk Fair.

TWO PHOTOGRAPHS OF MIDDLETON FAIR DAY in 1911 (above) and 1909 (below). One of the most important activities at fairs, before the advent of the motor car, was horse trading. Here the horses are being put through their paces before an expert and critical crowd. The fair was also a great social occasion especially for the children.

ARD CASTLE : MARKET PLACE.

AS WELL AS THE OCCASIONAL FAIRS there were the regular weekly markets of which that at Barnard Castle is the only survivor. Essentially the scene has changed little from that shown on this photograph of c. 1910.

FOR MANY YEARS the annual Barnard Castle Cyclists Meet on Whit Monday was one of the major social events of the year, attracting many spectators and entries from cycling clubs all over the North. Here the Committee and officials of the meet pose in the castle grounds.

A FEATURE OF THE ANNUAL CYCLISTS' MEET was the number of competitions for visiting clubs, including prizes for the best fancy dress costumes and for the club causing the most amusement. The Brunswick Cycling Club certainly ought to have been successful in one of these classes in 1913.

FROM THE 1880s ONWARDS THE ANNUAL AGRICULTURAL SHOW took the place of the fair as the social occasion of the year. As these photographs show it provided scope for rivalry in unexpected areas, with church and chapel competing for custom in their respective refreshment tents. The C of E ladies present a better-drilled and more uniform appearance but we do not know which was the more popular tent. Probably the men preferred the rival attractions of a beer tent. The sign on the Wesleyan tent reads: 'Tea with bread and butter and cake, 9 pence. Tea with ham sandwich, bread butter and cake 1 shilling'.

HIGH FORCE AND HOLWICK SHOW was too small for competition to be practicable and, in 1911 at least, the refreshment tent was non-denominational.

THE IMPORTANCE OF ORGANIZED FUNDRAISING in the days before the National Health Service is shown by these three photographs of demonstrations held in support of a local hospital. They are at Cotherstone (1910), Mickleton (1914), and Staindrop (undated but around the same time). In each case there is a procession with banners and bands, prominent local citizens, nurses, guides, schools and other organizations.

Hospital Demonstration. Mickleton. Nº3.

ANOTHER PROCESSION possibly for the same cause, though this time its purpose is not stated. It is in the mining village of Cockfield where the miners' lodge banner precedes the decorated floats.

THE THIRD DURHAM MILITIA PARADE in the market place, Barnard Castle, on their return from the South African War in 1901.

SOLDIERS OF THE TERRITORIALS marching through Staindrop in 1912.

AN ARMY RECRUITING SERGEANT on Middleton station with his first draft of recruits from the area in 1915.

BY THE END OF THE WAR there can have been few families whose life had not been touched by the loss of a relative or friend. The reunion of servicemen at Middleton in 1919 must have been an occasion of relief and of regret to all those taking part.

HOW MANY OF THE SPECTATORS AT THIS UNVEILING OF THE SOUTH AFRICAN WAR MEMORIAL would imagine that it would so soon be forgotten in the preparations for yet another war.

CELEBRATION OF KING'S CORONATION

THERE WERE OF COURSE MANY HAPPIER OCCASIONS to be celebrated. For the coronation of King Edward VII the festivities in Baldersdale were centred on the reservoir construction site where this large crowd assembled.

KING EDWARD had visited Teesdale before as the Prince of Wales (page 155) and did so on one or two occasions during his reign. Here a loyal, though not very numerous, crowd cheers his car as it crosses Barnard Castle bridge in 1907.

Building the Coronation Bonfire, Middleton. 1911.

THE CELEBRATIONS for the coronation of his successor, King George V, were also on a large scale with bonfires, like this one at Middleton, in nearly every village.

OTHER IMPORTANT OCCASIONS called for official photographs, like this one of the cutting of the first sod for the Blackton reservoir in 1889. Consider the problems faced by the photographer in posing some 200 people on a steep hillside and persuading all of them to stay still while he exposed the plate. It is remarkable that he succeeded so well.

THIS PARLIAMENTARY ELECTION of 1905 does not seem to have created much interest, if the scene outside the committee room of one of the candidates is typical. 'Vote Beaumont and the big loaf' reads the poster, but those present seem more interested in the car – a very rare sight at that date.

THIS ELECTION seems to have aroused rather more interest. A crowd is assembled to hear the returning officer, Mr J.l. Dawson (page 105), announce the result. The photograph is not dated but the election probably took place around 1930.

A VERY SERIOUS-LOOKING WEDDING GROUP in Baldersdale in the 1920s.

THE HARVEST FESTIVAL SCENE in the tiny chapel at Brisco in 1914.

THERE WERE MANY PRIVATE FAMILY OCCASIONS TO BE RECORDED, such as this christening party of the Milner family at Charity Farm, Bowes, around 1887. It seems a very solemn occasion.

AFTER THE END OF THE GROUSE-SHOOTING SEASON, it was customary for the landowner and/or shooting tenant to give a dinner for game-keepers and beaters. This undated photograph shows such an annual dinner at the shooting box at Holwick.

Mechanics' Ball 1912

DURING THE WINTER MONTHS whist drives and dances were common village entertainments usually with some charitable fund-raising in view. Often both were held in the same building – normally the village school if there was no hall – with the dance following the more serious business of whist. The most prestigious event in the upper dale was the New Year's Eve Ball organized by the Mechanics Institute.

Holwick Dance, Juny 30th 1914.

Mickleton Whist Drive & Dance. Nov 1st

THREE MUCH MORE DRAMATIC INCIDENTS FOLLOW. The first is a fire at the village of Cotherstone on a site now occupied by the garage and petrol station. It can be seen that the building had a thatched roof and it was apparently this which caught fire.

THE SCENE OUTSIDE A BARNARD CASTLE SHOP after the tradesman had refused to accede to an order by the Town Council to remove a new shop window which he had installed without permission. The gun, which had been a relic of the South African War, was installed in front of the shop by some local joker to show that the Council meant business.

'TURNED TURTLE' says this 1920 photograph, with a rueful group surveying the wreckage of a traction engine at Etherley. The incident does not appear to have been reported in the local newspaper. As early as 1871 the Raby Estates had bought two Fowler steam engines for the use of their tenants and from then on, though never common, traction engines were in use in the lower part of the dale.

Visitors

ONE OF THE MOST UNEXPECTED VISITORS to Teesdale must have been the pilot of this RAF plane which landed in March 1917 on the Demesnes. It was on the way from Glasgow to the south and the *Teesdale Mercury* reported '. . . was the object of much curious attention, a large crowd witnessing its departure the following morning . . .'.

SCOTT'S CAVE on the banks of the River Greta at Rokeby. Sir Walter Scott was a friend of J.B.S. Morritt of Rokeby and stayed there on several occasions while writing his long romantic poem *Rokeby* which did so much to popularize Teesdale. It is said that Scott used this cave as a retreat and that it is the one which figures largely in the poem.

ANOTHER REASON FOR VISITING TEESDALE can be seen in this atmospheric photograph by E. Yeoman. There were several chalybeate springs in the dale and attempts were made in the nineteenth century to promote Teesdale as a health resort. This shows the spa at Gainford. An interesting footnote for those contemplating a return to 'Victorian values' is that the spas at Gainford and Barnard Castle were reportedly 'wantonly destroyed' in 1871. Vandalism is not only a modern phenomenon.

THE MILITIA TERRITORIALS AND REGULAR ARMY were frequent visitors to Teesdale and especially to Barnard Castle, from the middle of the nineteenth century until after the Second World War. This parade in the market place is undated; nor is it clear whether the men are local volunteers. Judging by the number of boys present, perhaps they are.

THIS, ON THE OTHER HAND, IS DATED and is very much an official souvenir photograph. It shows the officers of the Durham Militia in the castle during their training camp in 1864.

DURING THE SECOND WORLD WAR Barnard Castle and district became an important army training area. These photographs show Winston Churchill with Duncan Sandys and a group of senior officers watching from Whorlton Bridge, as troops practice river crossings and scaling cliffs.

THIS LITTLE GROUP OF BELGIAN REFUGEES, sent to Middleton during the First World War, must have helped to bring home to the people of Teesdale the unpleasant fact that things were changing and would never be the same again.

A GROWING FLOOD OF EMIGRANTS left Teesdale usually for the USA or Canada from around 1870 onwards. Such an important movement could not go unrecorded here: in the absence of any old photograph it was decided to include this picture of the still extant log cabin built by Teesdale emigrants as a school house in the remote Shirley Basin area of Wyoming.

MANY OTHER VISITORS TO TEESDALE over the years did not come from choice but because of their parents' wishes. The Barnard Castle School was founded in 1886 as the North Eastern Counties School.

THE ARRIVAL OF THE RAILWAY meant a great increase in the number of visitors to Teesdale. Though the line terminated at Middleton, several proprietors ran brakes, like this one, to and from the station especially to High Force. Two horses would not have been too many to haul the brake and its 15 occupants up some of the hills. The photograph was probably taken in the early years of this century.

THE ADVENT OF THE RAILWAY made it much easier for shooting parties like this one, though not often so distinguished, to reach the moors. Here is the Prince of Wales' (later Edward VII) party outside High Force Hotel on 15 August 1866. In the centre is HRH, very much the well dressed sportsman, though the rest of the party could easily be taken for an amateur dramatic society. The gentleman on the extreme left is Mr Scarth, agent for the Duke of Cleveland. Note how carefully the photographer has posed the picture to show that the agent, though with the party, is definitely not of it. The visit was the occasion of unbelievably sycophantic letters and articles in the local press.

A LATER AND MUCH MORE RELAXED PICTURE of a shooting party at Riggside, Harwood, c. 1905. Mr Scarth (third from the left) is very much in evidence rather than being an adjunct to the party. Perhaps formality was relaxed as photography became more usual and almost certainly the absence of royalty helped in this case.

AS THE MOORS BECAME MORE ACCESSIBLE TO SHOOTING PARTIES more attention was given to their accommodation. The shooting on the Earl of Strathmore's land at Holwick was let to Cosmo Bonsor Esq. MP, a director of the Bank of England who decided to build a shooting box there. The photograph shows building in progress in 1890. One of the workers was Richard Watson who suffered the accident there which was to end his life. The builders were Hubbards of London.

ANOTHER SHOOTING BOX was Wemmergill Hall in Lunedale, used by the Milbank family. Relaxing in the smoking room here in 1872 are Mr F.A. Milbank, Mr P. Milbank, Mr Seton Stewart and Revd F. Byng. On 22 August of that year six guns accounted for 2,070 grouse on the Wemmergill moor.

AMONG THE VERY EARLY VISITORS TO TEESDALE were the Romans, though their presence seems to have been largely confined to the forts at Greta Bridge and Bowes. This building inscription was erected around AD 205 presumably to mark some rebuilding work at Greta Bridge fort. It named the Emperor Severns and his two sons, Antonious Pius and Geta. However, Geta was later murdered by his brother and his name removed from this and all other monuments. The slab was found in 1793 at the back of the present Morritt Arms hotel and was removed by the landowners, the Eden family, to their home at Windlestone Hall where this photograph was taken in the 1920s. The stone has since been restored to Teesdale and is on display in the Bowes Museum.

THE MAJOR MONUMENTS IN TEESDALE, the Bronze Age cairn at Kirk Arran and the stone circle at Egglestone, were destroyed before photography could record them – other minor monuments and artefacts were more fortunate. The Anglian memorial stone was found at Wycliffe in the eighteenth century, but was subsequently lost sight of and only rediscovered by the then curator of The Bowes Museum, Mr Sydney Harrison in 1936. For safekeeping it was fixed to an inner wall in the Hall and remained there until 1984 when it was quietly removed by a new owner of the Hall and offered for sale in London. Fortunately it was recognized in the sale room by a dealer who bought it and immediately offered it to the Bowes Museum where it is now displayed.

ROMAN REMAINS continued to be discovered. One of the most important finds in Teesdale was of two Roman shrines to the god Vinotonus Silvanus, high on Scargill Moor. The photograph, taken in 1946, shows one of the shrines with a large altar still in place. It was later removed to the Bowes Museum. Standing round are the excavators. From left to right they are: Mr T. Wake, curator of the Bowes Museum, and three noted Roman scholars, Professor Ian Richmond, Mr F.G. Simpson and Mr R.P. Wright.

ACKNOWLEDGEMENTS

The author is pleased to acknowledge the invaluable help which has been kindly given by the following individuals and organizations who have lent photographs and supplied information:

Mr H.L. Beadle • Beamish Museum • Mrs H. Bendelow • Mrs R. Blenkinsop
The Bowes Museum • Mr and Mrs H. Cross • Mr A. Douglas
Durham County Museums Education Service • The Gaunless Valley Trust,
especially Mr M. Makepeace and Mr K. Richardson • Mrs L.D. Headlam-Morley
Mr O. Hedley • Mr B. Hutchinson • Mr and Mrs E. Kaye • the Parish Councils of
Teesdale District • Sir Mark Milbank • Northumbrian Water Authority
Mrs Betty Raine • Mr E. Raine • Mr H. Sayer • Mr M.J. Stow
Teesdale Record Society, especially Mr P. Raine • Mr F.S. Todd • Mr W. Townson
Mr J. Winter.

Any merit which this work has is due to them. Errors and omissions are entirely the responsibility of the author.